Crochet Dishcloth
15 Colorful And Pretty Crochet Dishcloth Patterns To Brighten Your Kitchen

Disclamer: All photos used in this book, including the cover photo were made available under a Attribution-ShareAlike 2.0 Generic (CC BY-SA 2.0)

and sourced from Flickr

Copyright 2016 by DONATAS TSITSENAS - All rights reserved.

This document is geared towards providing exact and reliable information in regards to the topic and issue covered. The publication is sold with the idea that the publisher is not required to render accounting, officially permitted, or otherwise, qualified services. If advice is necessary, legal or professional, a practiced individual in the profession should be ordered.

- From a Declaration of Principles which was accepted and approved equally by a Committee of the American Bar Association and a Committee of Publishers and Associations.

In no way is it legal to reproduce, duplicate, or transmit any part of this document in either electronic means or in printed format. Recording of this publication is strictly prohibited and any storage of this document is not allowed unless with written permission from the publisher. All rights reserved.

The information provided herein is stated to be truthful and consistent, in that any liability, in terms of inattention or otherwise, by any usage or abuse of any policies, processes, or directions contained within is the solitary and utter responsibility of the recipient reader. Under no circumstances will any legal responsibility or blame be held against the publisher for any reparation, damages, or monetary loss due to the information herein, either directly or indirectly.

Respective authors own all copyrights not held by the publisher.

The information herein is offered for informational purposes solely, and is universal as so. The presentation of the information is without contract or any type of guarantee assurance.

The trademarks that are used are without any consent, and the publication of the trademark is without permission or backing by the trademark owner. All trademarks and brands within this book are for clarifying purposes only and are the owned by the owners themselves, not affiliated with this document.

Table of content

Introduction..6

Chapter 1 – Getting Started 9

Chapter 2 – Your First Dishcloths 12

Easy Peasy Dishcloth..12

White as Snow Dishcloth 14

All About Those Waves Dishcloth 15

The Black and White Classics Dishcloth 17

Chapter 3 – Bringing In Your Style 19

Be My Valentine Dishcloths 19

The Spring Mix Dishcloth 21

The Happy Rainbow Dishcloth 23

Fun and Flirty Dishcloths 25

Chapter 4 – The Jazzy Section 27

Triple Crochet Border Dishcloth 27

Summer Patriot Dishcloths 29

Muted Moss Dishcloths 31

Chapter 5 – Variation Patterns 33

The Self Striper Dishcloths 34

The Triple Crochet Self Striper Dishcloth (Photo Above) 35

Storm Cloud Dishcloth 36

The Open Work Storm Cloud Dishcloth (Photo Above) 37

Conclusion 40

Introduction

There you are, browsing the aisles of the store once again, trying to find that one perfect set of cloths to put in your kitchen. You know what you want, but you just can't seem to find it on the shelves of the store, no matter how hard you look.

You could order online, but those are expensive, and you still aren't getting quite the look that you want. You want something that is new. Something that is fresh. Something that is unique to you and you alone, but all you can find are those same old patterns you see in your friend's houses.

You want something that represents you and your style. It's your kitchen, and you want to feel like you are expressing yourself while you are in it. You want to show off your flare to the world while you bake and cook, and to do that, you have to have the right tools for the job.

So, you simply are going to have to make it yourself.

"But I don't know if I can. These look hard."

"I have never made anything crocheted before... could I do it?"

"I want to make something by hand, but they look too difficult for what I have the time for… how can I make this work?"

If you have ever felt any of these things, you are not alone, but trust me, crochet is an easy hobby that you are going to fall in love with. The twisting and turning of the yarn is not only fun, but it's relaxing.

Unwind from your day with your favorite beverage and your favorite color yarn, and settle in to create and express yourself as often as you would like. You are going to end up with projects that show off your style, and you are going to amaze your friends and family with all of the pieces you are able to create.

So if you are done with browsing the stores, trying to find the unique items that you know you will only get if you make them yourself, you have come to the right place. Let me show you the wonderful world of crochet, and let me help you step into the land of arts and crafts.

You are going to open the door to complete creative freedom, and you are going to be free to make anything you like, whenever you like.

Are you ready to dive into a whole new world?

Good.

Let's get started.

Chapter 1 – Getting Started

Getting started with crochet can be both fun and intimidating if you have never done it before, but I am going to make it easy for you.

Here is a guide on how to create the stitches you are going to find in this book. They are all incredibly simply to create, you just have to practice them to perfect them.

Follow the directions, then dive into the patterns. You will be amazed at how easy they are!

Foundation chain – the foundation chain is the beginning of any crochet project. To create one, you are going to make a slip knot on the yarn, with a length hanging down. This length is going to be trimmed off when you are done.

Slip the knot over the hook and pull it firmly against the hook. To create a chain, grab the yarn with the hook, and pull it through the loop. You now have another loop on the hook, and a loop in the yarn beneath the hook. This is a chain.

When you see in a pattern that you must chain 10, you are going to continue this sequence until you have 10 of these loops on the yarn itself.

Single crochet – chain 10 for your foundation chain. To single crochet, you are going to wrap the yarn up and over the back, then push the hook through the center of the first chain next to the hook. Grab the yarn, and pull it through this loop.

Wrap the yarn up and over the hook, and pull it through the first loop you still have on your hook. Wrap it over once more, then pull it through the final loop.

This is your single crochet stitch. Repeat the sequence across the row.

Double crochet – chain 10 once more, only this time, you are going to wrap the yarn around 2 times. Push it through the center of the loop, and grab the yarn.

Pull it through, then wrap the yarn up and over the hook, and pull it through the first loop you still have on your hook. Wrap it over once more, then pull it through the next loop.

Bring the yarn up and over from the back one final time, and pull it through the last loop on the hook.

This is your double crochet. Repeat across the row.

Triple crochet – for triple crochet, chain 10.

Wrap the yarn around the hook 3 times. Push the hook through the center of the loop, and pull it through. Bring the yarn up and over, and pull it through the first loop on the hook.

Bring the yarn up and over again, and repeat. Do this again, then once more for the final loops on the hook.

This is your triple crochet. As you can see, the single, double, and triple are all referring to how many times you wrap the yarn around the hook, then how many times you need to pull it through to create your stitch. You can apply this to get any number of stitches you like.

Front loop only – as you have noticed, as you crochet, each stitch has 2 loops.

When you are crocheting in the front loop only, you are pushing the hook through the center of these 2 loops instead of sliding it under them.

The front loop is the loop facing the front of the project. You are always going to use this loop with front loop only.

That's it! These are the only stitches you need to know for these projects. Practice them with the dishcloths, and you are going to be a master in no time.

Chapter 2 – Your First Dishcloths

It's finally time to get started! Take your time through each of these patterns, and keep an eye on your tension. Make sure you are pulling the yarn consistently the same throughout the cloth so you end up with a square.

You can follow the same colors that I chose, or you can use your own colors, just make sure you choose cotton yarn. Cotton comes in all kinds of colors, it's not expensive, and it's easy on the hands. Use this for all of your dishcloths and kitchen needs, and you will never want to use anything else again.

Easy Peasy Dishcloth

Photo made by: gillicious

You will need 1 ball of yarn in the color of your choice and a size G crochet hook

Chain a length that is 6 inches long.

Single crochet across the row. Chain 1, turn, and single crochet back to the beginning. Chain 1, turn, and single crochet across the row.

For row 3, chain 1, turn, and single crochet in the front loop only across the row. Chain 1, turn, and single crochet in the front loop only across the row once more.

For row 5, chain 1, turn, and single crochet normally across the row. Chain 1, turn, and single crochet normally back to the other side.

For row 7, chain 1, turn, and single crochet in the front loop only across the row. Chain 1, turn, and single crochet in the front loop only across the row once more.

Continue with this same pattern now, alternating between regular single crochet and front loop only single crochet every two rows. When you have a square, you are ready for the border.

For the border, you are going to single crochet across the row, then continue to single crochet down one side, across the bottom, and up the other side. Join with a slip stitch, and tie off.

That's it! You now have your first dishcloth.

White as Snow Dishcloth

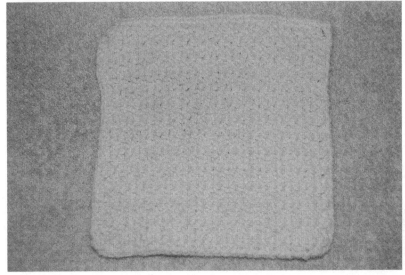

Photo made by: Twanda Baker

You will need 1 ball of yarn in white of your choice and a size G crochet hook

Chain a length that is 6 inches long.

Chain 1, turn, and single crochet back to the beginning. Chain 1, turn, and single crochet back across the row.

Chain 1, turn, and single crochet back to the beginning. Chain 1, turn, and single crochet across the row.

You are going to repeat this same pattern now, always chaining 1 at the end of each row before you turn and begin again. Make sure your tension stays the same throughout, but make sure you keep the tension nice and snug. Continue to work until you have a square.

For the border, you are going to single crochet across the row, then continue to single crochet down one side, across the bottom, and up the other side. Join with a slip stitch, and tie off.

That's it! Your dishcloth is ready for work.

All About Those Waves Dishcloth

Photo made by: Stylva

You will need 1 ball of yarn in the color of your choice and a size G crochet hook

Chain a length that is 6 inches long.

Single crochet across the row. Chain 1, turn.

Single crochet in the first 4 stitches, then double crochet in the next 4 stitches. Single crochet in the next 4 stitches, then double crochet in the next 4 stitches.

Repeat this across the row, making sure you finish with a single crochet stitch. Chain 1, turn.

Single crochet in the first 4 stitches, then double crochet in the next 4 stitches. Single crochet in the next 4 stitches, then double crochet in the next 4 stitches.

Chain 1, turn, and repeat the pattern.

You are going to continue with this same pattern until you have a square.

Leave a raw edge on this border.

The Black and White Classics Dishcloth

Photo made by: becky bokern

You will need 1 ball of yarn in black and one in white and a size G crochet hook

Chain a length that is 6 inches long.

Chain 2, turn, and double crochet back to the beginning. Chain 2, turn, and double crochet back across the row.

Chain 2, turn, and double crochet back to the beginning. Chain 2, turn, and double crochet across the row.

You are going to repeat this same pattern now, always chaining 2 at the end of each row before you turn and begin again. Make sure your tension stays the same throughout, and continue to work until you have a square.

Tie off, then add the border.

For the border, join with the opposite color. Single crochet across the row, then continue to single crochet down one side, across the bottom, and up the other side. Join with a slip stitch, and tie off.

For variations in the look, try following the same pattern using either single crochet or triple crochet.

That's it!

Chapter 3 – Bringing In Your Style

Whether you want to celebrate your favorite time of year, you want to bring in your own favorite colors, or you are looking for something that is classy yet refined, you are sure to find the dishcloth you need here.

Use the same colors I used, or choose your own for your own original look. No matter how you do it, you are going to love the results.

Be My Valentine Dishcloths

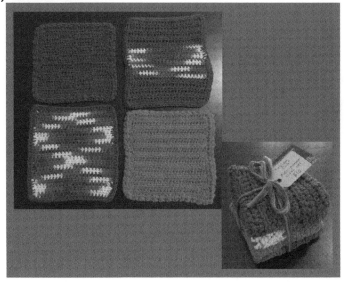

Photo made by: becky bokern

You will need 1 ball of yarn in the color of your choice and a size G crochet hook

Chain a length that is 6 inches long.

Chain 2, turn, and double crochet back to the beginning. Chain 2, turn, and double crochet back across the row.

Chain 2, turn, and double crochet back to the beginning. Chain 2, turn, and double crochet across the row.

You are going to repeat this same pattern now, always chaining 2 at the end of each row before you turn and begin again. Make sure your tension stays the same throughout, and continue to work until you have a square.

For the border, you are going to single crochet across the row, then continue to single crochet down one side, across the bottom, and up the other side. Join with a slip stitch, and tie off.

If you want to have the alternating stripe, work this pattern for 2 inches, then change colors to your stripe. Follow the pattern for another 2 inches, before you tie off and go back to your main color.

That's it!

The Spring Mix Dishcloth

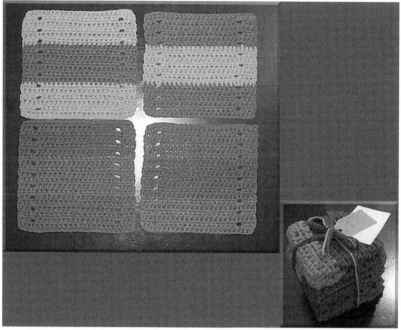

Photo made by: becky bokern

You will need 2 balls of yarn in the 2 colors of your choice and a size G crochet hook

Chain a length that is 6 inches long. Chain 2, and double crochet across the row.

Chain 2, turn, and double crochet in the first 3 stitches. Chain 4, skip the next 2 stitches, and double crochet in the next stitch. Continue to double crochet until you are 5 stitches away from the end of the row.

Chain 4, skip the next 2 stitches, and double crochet in the last 3 stitches.

For the next row, chain 2, turn, and double crochet in the first 3 stitches. Chain 4, skip the next 2 stitches, and double crochet in the next stitch. Continue to double crochet until you are 5 stitches away from the end of the row.

Chain 4, skip the next 2 stitches, and double crochet in the last 3 stitches.

Repeat this pattern until you are 2 inches up the side of the cloth.

Change colors now, and join with a slip stitch.

Chain 2, turn, and double crochet in the first 3 stitches. Chain 4, skip the next 2 stitches, and double crochet in the next stitch. Continue to double crochet until you are 5 stitches away from the end of the row.

Chain 4, skip the next 2 stitches, and double crochet in the last 3 stitches.

Repeat this pattern until you have a 2 inch stripe, then go back to your first color.

Chain 2, turn, and double crochet in the first 3 stitches. Chain 4, skip the next 2 stitches, and double crochet in the next stitch. Continue to double crochet until you are 5 stitches away from the end of the row.

Chain 4, skip the next 2 stitches, and double crochet in the last 3 stitches.

Leave a raw edge on this border.

The Happy Rainbow Dishcloth

Photo made by: Lisa Plummer

You will need 1 ball of yarn in the color of your choice and a size G crochet hook

Chain 5, and join with a slip stitch to form a ring.

Single crochet in the center of this stitch 12 times. Chain 2, and turn.

Double crochet in the first 3 stitches, chain 5, and double crochet in the next 3 stitches. Chain 5, double crochet in the next 3 stitches, chain 5, and double crochet in the next 3 stitches.

Join with a slip stitch and chain 2. Double crochet in each of the stitches around, double crochet in the chain space 2 times, chain 2, and double crochet in the same space 2 times. Repeat this around.

Chain 2, turn, and double crochet in each of the stitches. When you reach the chain space, you are going to double crochet in it 1 time, chain 2, and double crochet in it once more. Repeat around.

Continue to follow this pattern until you have a square that is 6 inches tall by 6 inches wide. You are now ready to add the border.

For the border, you are going to single crochet across the row, then continue to single crochet down one side, across the bottom, and up the other side. Join with a slip stitch, and tie off.

That's it! You're done!

Fun and Flirty Dishcloths

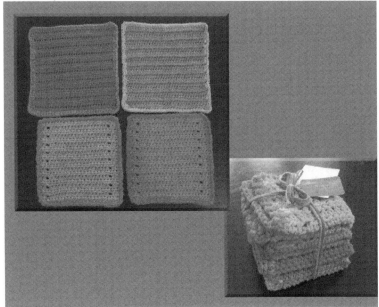

Photo made by: becky bokern

You will need 2 balls of yarn in the 2 colors of your choice and a size G crochet hook

Chain a length that is 6 inches long.

Chain 2, turn, and double crochet back to the beginning. Chain 2, turn, and double crochet back across the row.

Chain 2, turn, and double crochet back to the beginning. Chain 2, turn, and double crochet across the row.

You are going to repeat this same pattern now, always chaining 2 at the end of each row before you turn and begin again. Make sure your tension stays the same throughout, and continue to work until you have a square.

Tie off, then add the border.

You are going to use a different color, and join with a slip stitch. Single crochet across the top, then continue to single crochet down one side, across the bottom, and up the other side. Join with a slip stitch, and tie off.

Please note: If you want to have the open work ends, follow the directions for the spring mix crochet cloths, but use these colors.

Chapter 4 – The Jazzy Section

Whether you are feeling a little classic, a little funky, or a little jazzy, there is something in this chapter for you. Have fun with the patterns, have fun with the colors, and give your kitchen that pop it's been waiting for!

Triple Crochet Border Dishcloth

Photo made by: Lisa Plummer

You will need 1 ball of yarn in the color of your choice and a size G crochet hook

Chain a length that is 6 inches long.

Chain 1, turn, and single crochet back to the beginning. Chain 1, turn, and single crochet back across the row.

Chain 1, turn, and single crochet back to the beginning. Chain 1, turn, and single crochet across the row.

You are going to repeat this same pattern now, always chaining 1 at the end of each row before you turn and begin again. Make sure your tension stays the same throughout, and continue to work until you have a square.

Tie off, and change to another color for the border.

For the border, you are going to join with a slip stitch, and chain 3. Triple crochet across the top of the cloth, then continue to triple crochet down one side, across the bottom, and up the other side. Join with a slip stitch, and tie off.

Summer Patriot Dishcloths

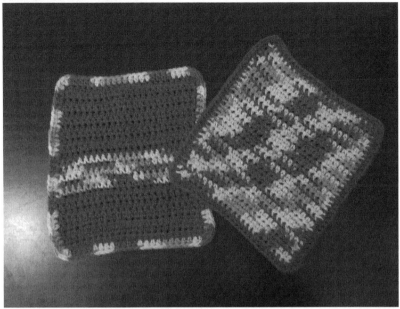

Photo made by: becky bokern

You will need 2 balls of yarn in the colors of your choice and a size G crochet hook

Chain a length that is 6 inches long.

Chain 2, turn, and double crochet back to the beginning. Chain 2, turn, and double crochet back across the row.

Chain 2, turn, and double crochet back to the beginning. Chain 2, turn, and double crochet across the row.

You are going to repeat this same pattern now, always chaining 2 at the end of each row before you turn and begin again. Make sure your tension stays the same throughout, and continue to work until you have a square.

Tie off, then add the border.

You are going to use a different color, and join with a slip stitch. Single crochet across the top, then continue to single crochet down one side, across the bottom, and up the other side. Join with a slip stitch, and tie off.

Please note: If you want to create a cloth with the stripe on one side, you are going to complete 5 rows, tie off, and join a different color with a slip stitch. Repeat the pattern for another 3 rows, before you tie off and go back to your main color.

Muted Moss Dishcloths

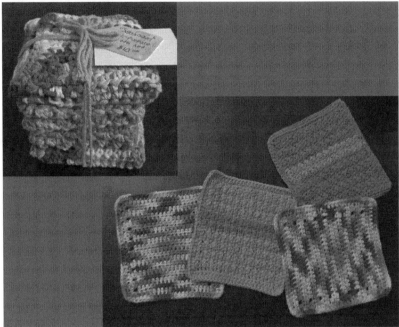

Photo made by: becky bokern

You will need 1 ball of yarn in the color of your choice and a size G crochet hook

Chain a length that is 6 inches long.

Chain 2, turn, and double crochet back to the beginning. Chain 2, turn, and double crochet back across the row.

Chain 2, turn, and double crochet back to the beginning. Chain 2, turn, and double crochet across the row.

You are going to repeat this same pattern now, always chaining 2 at the end of each row before you turn and begin again. Make sure your tension stays the same throughout, and continue to work until you have a square.

For the border, you are going to single crochet across the row, then continue to single crochet down one side, across the bottom, and up the other side. Join with a slip stitch, and tie off.

Please note: If you want to create a cloth with the stripe on one side, you are going to complete 5 rows, tie off, and join a different color with a slip stitch. Repeat the pattern for another 3 rows, before you tie off and go back to your main color.

That's it!

Chapter 5 – Variation Patterns

Here are a few patterns that show you how to use a single ball of yarn to get two entirely different looks for a washcloth.

First, you are going to use single crochet, then you are going to use triple, and the result is an entirely different outcome. Later on you will see the difference between a double crochet cloth from an open work cloth.

Make these patterns, then try mixing it up by throwing in variations with the stitches you are using. You can even change the border by using double crochet instead of single, or even alternating between single and double as you go along.

The point is to have fun, and let your imagination run wild!

The Self Striper Dishcloths

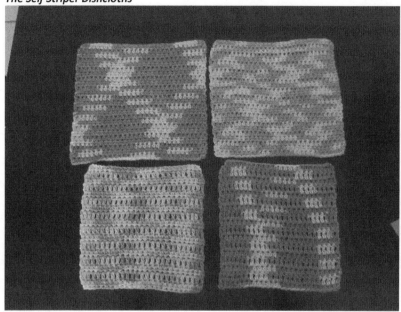

Photo made by: becky bokern

You will need 1 ball of yarn in the color of your choice and a size G crochet hook

Chain a length that is 6 inches long.

Chain 1, turn, and single crochet back to the beginning. Chain 1, turn, and single crochet back across the row.

Chain 1, turn, and single crochet back to the beginning. Chain 1, turn, and single crochet across the row.

You are going to repeat this same pattern now, always chaining 1 at the end of each row before you turn and begin again. Make sure your tension stays the same throughout, and continue to work until you have a square.

For the border, you are going to single crochet across the row, then continue to single crochet down one side, across the bottom, and up the other side. Join with a slip stitch, and tie off.

That's it! You're all set!

The Triple Crochet Self Striper Dishcloth (Photo Above)
You will need 1 ball of yarn in the color of your choice and a size G crochet hook

Chain a length that is 6 inches long.

Chain 3, turn, and triple crochet back to the beginning. Chain 3, turn, and triple crochet back across the row.

Chain 3, turn, and triple crochet back to the beginning. Chain 3, turn, and triple crochet across the row.

You are going to repeat this same pattern now, always chaining 3 at the end of each row before you turn and begin again. Make sure your tension stays the same throughout, and continue to work until you have a square.

For the border, you are going to single crochet across the row, then continue to single crochet down one side, across the bottom, and up the other side. Join with a slip stitch, and tie off.

That's it!

Storm Cloud Dishcloth

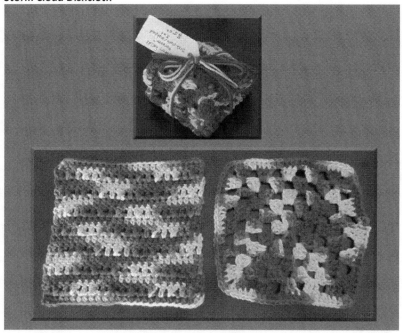

Photo made by: becky bokern

You will need 1 ball of yarn in the color of your choice and a size G crochet hook

Chain a length that is 6 inches long.

Chain 2, turn, and double crochet back to the beginning. Chain 2, turn, and double crochet back across the row.

Chain 2, turn, and double crochet back to the beginning. Chain 2, turn, and double crochet across the row.

You are going to repeat this same pattern now, always chaining 2 at the end of each row before you turn and begin again. Make sure your tension stays the same throughout, and continue to work until you have a square.

For the border, you are going to single crochet across the row, then continue to single crochet down one side, across the bottom, and up the other side. Join with a slip stitch, and tie off.

That's it! Your dishcloth is ready for action.

The Open Work Storm Cloud Dishcloth (Photo Above)
You will need 1 ball of yarn in the color of your choice and a size G crochet hook

Chain 5, and join with a slip stitch to form a ring.

Single crochet in the center of this stitch 12 times. Chain 2, and turn.

Double crochet in the first 3 stitches, chain 5, and double crochet in the next 3 stitches. Chain 5, double crochet in the next 3 stitches, chain 5, and double crochet in the next 3 stitches.

Chain 2, and double crochet in the chain space 4 times. Chain 3, and double crochet in the chain space 4 times. Chain 5, and skip the next 3, then double crochet in the chain space 4 times. Chain 5, and skip the next 3, and double crochet in the chain space 4 times.

Chain 2, and double crochet in the chain space 4 times. Chain 3, and double crochet in the chain space 4 times. Chain 5, and skip the next 3, then double crochet in the chain space 4 times. Chain 5, and skip the next 3, and double crochet in the chain space 4 times.

Continue this pattern around the other two corners.

Chain 2, and repeat the entire sequence once more. You are going to continue to group the double crochets in the chain spaces you create, and you are going to consistently chain 5, then skip the next 3 stitches to create more chain spaces.

Continue to work until you have a square that is 6 inches wide and 6 inches tall. You are now ready to add on the border.

For the border, you are going to single crochet across the row, then continue to single crochet down one side, across the bottom, and up the other side. Join with a slip stitch, and tie off.

That's it! Enjoy!

Conclusion

There you have it, everything you need to get started in crochet, and exactly what you need to create your very first dishcloths.

I hope this book was able to inspire you to create the items you want to put in your kitchen, and that you were able to ease into the world of crochet with the fun that this hobby provides. I know it can be frustrating at first, but I encourage you to stick with it.

The more you practice, the easier it's going to get, and the better you are going to be with each and every project.

I know you can do it, and I want you to get comfortable enough to branch out and try your own style. Throw in a bit of flare here, add in a touch of you there. You never know how many things you can modify and create until you try, and once you do, you will be hooked for life.

This book is designed for the beginner, so don't worry if you think you need to practice before you move on to more advanced projects. You can create these dishcloths at any level, and the more you practice, the easier they are going to get.

Have fun with it, and mix and match the stitches. See how many ways you can make the same dishcloth look different, and how many ways you can get the yarn to change based on the stitches you are using. Have fun with the entire process, and there won't be anything that is too hard for you.

I hope you enjoyed learning how to crochet, and I hope you take your skills to the next level. This is a hobby that is going to serve you well no matter how old you are, what you enjoy doing, or what kinds of projects you want to make.

Dive into the world of crochet, and enjoy the entire process. No project is going to be too hard.

Happy crocheting!

Made in United States
Orlando, FL
31 March 2024